i should have given them water

i should have given them water

Poems

Eileen Malone

Ragged Sky Press
Princeton, New Jersey

Copyright © 2010 by Eileen Malone

Published by Ragged Sky Press
PO Box 312
Annandale, NJ 08801

All rights reserved. No part of this book may be reproduced or transmitted in any form or by any means without written permission of the author.

Library of Congress Cataloging-in-Publication Data
Malone, Eileen, 1944-
I should have given them water : poems / Eileen Malone. -- 1st ed.
p. cm.
ISBN 978-1-933974-08-8 (pbk. : alk. paper)
I. Title.
PS3613.A4625I3 2010
811'.6--dc22
                                                    2010010220

This book is composed in Adobe Garamond and Ariel
Cover design by Eileen Malone
Cover artwork: *Stylized Flowers in Front of a Decorative Background* (1908), still life by Egon Schiele
Author photograph by Robert DeKraker
Graphic and layout consultant: Az Samad

Manufactured in the United States of America

First Edition

ACKNOWLEDGMENTS

Grateful acknowledgment is made to the following in which some of the poems in this volume first appeared, several in slightly different forms with different titles, and to the judges of their competitions who awarded same.

Publications:
Litchfield Review; Bent Pin Quarterly; Thunder Sandwich; The River, Natchez Poetry Anthology; An Eye for an Eye Makes the Whole World Blind—Poets on 9/11; Icarus; So To Speak; Mannequin Envy; Gallery of Erotica Readers and Writers Association; SLAB, SoMa Literary Review; Mudfish; Southern Poetry Review; Saucy Vox; Cezanne's Carrot; The Typewriter; Black Mountain Review

Awards:
Madison Review's Phyllis Smart Young Prize; *Harpur Palate*, HM; *Abiko Quarterly* (Japan), Second Prize; *Country Mouse*, HM, *Penumbra*, Second Prize and HM; *Potpourri*, RunnerUp and Finalist; *Haight-Ashbury Literary Journal*, Second Prize; *Spoon River Poetry Review*, Editors Prize, Finalist; *Americas Review*, Finalist, *Half Tones to Jubilee*, First Prize; *Confluence*, Second Prize; *Comstock Review*, Finalist; *Banyan Review*, First Prize; *Lucidity*, First Prize; *Bellingham Review*, Semifinalist; Dorothy Daniels Writing Award, First Prize; *Anhinga*'s Cynthia Cahn Prize, Second Prize; Milford Fine Arts Council, First Prize and Second Prize; *Mindfire Renewed*, Second Prize; *Ariel*, First Prize; *Grandmother Earth*, Second Prize; *Acorn*, First Prize; *Peregrine*, Second Prize; *Noe Valley Voice*, HM; Pen Women (National), First Prize, Second Prize' Sacramento Poetry Center, HM; Virginia R. Murray Award, First Prize; Emily Powell Literary Memorial, First Prize.

Also, very warm thanks to Ellen Foos and Vasiliki Katsarou for appreciating my poetry enough to publish it as well as their generous editorial care and assistance with this book, without whom. . . .

CONTENTS

Acknowledgments   v

PART ONE

More Like Angels   1
What It Is to Gamble   2
Girl Mothering   3
Melon   4
Where We Have Been   5
Lacemaker   6
Without Any Intention   7
We Wait   8
Spokes of a Wheel   9
Cool, Damp Peace   10
Peach Pit   11
Potato Eyes   12
He Wants to Let Himself Go   13
Calliope   14
This One Hit, This Sniff   15
Fish Don't Mourn   16
Visiting Day   17
She Takes Off Her Clothes   18

PART TWO

Muscle and Slur   21
Raga   22
Man with a Birthmark   23
Scattering   24
Man with Easter Island Head   25
Ash Tuesday   26
Departure   27
As Long as Is Necessary   28
Wharf Without Purpose   29

Around You   30
Something Very Uncomfortable   31
A Certain Pink Cry   33
Dove Meat   34
Grandmother Spider   35
Newly Divorced   36
Not My Umbrella   37
Hacker   38
Lost Lot of Us   39
He Must Like Prison   40
Hug   41

PART THREE

She Kisses Steam   45
Convalescent Conversation   46
Your Old Housefly   47
Shine of My Own Relief   48
Overnight in the Lighthouse   49
Wild Sugar   50
Bougainvillea   51
Waltz   52
Her Good Hearth   53
These Things, That Others Might Call Miracles   54
The Ponderous Falls from Her   55
Wild Glass   56
As a Trobriand Islander Harvests Yams   57
Antique Shop   58
The Way Our Dreams Swam in Sync   59
In Time, Even Ghosts Can Heal   61
Not the First Unbeliever: 1. Sedona   62
Not the First Unbeliever: 2. The Wedding   63
Not the First Unbeliever: 3. Fireboat   64
Otherthings   65
Parakeet Expectations   66
Insinuation of Wings   67
Aquaria   68

PART ONE

MORE LIKE ANGELS

Again, I retreat to another
aspirin-white public bathroom
where the scent of pine is denser than that of urine
and everything has been stolen
that anyone thought worth stealing

stand by the toilet, swig vodka
the only thing I have available to cheat this fear
that comes on me like pain, information
hope is no more than a nightlight
for children, before rehab, before addiction
before God became Santa Claus
and my soul became money-driven
before hurt was all I could do
I've spent most of my life unredeemed

stilettos clack on tile into the bathroom stall
on one side of mine; I see butterflies tattooed
on high-heeled ankles no more than syllables
hear her sniff, snort, try to cover it up with a cough

all my good intentions pool into a puddle
of myself at my feet, I flush, swing open the door
wash my hands in the sink, inhale steam
from someone else's paper cup of black coffee

pick up her lipstick-smeared unfiltered cigarette
that smolders on the counter edge, take a drag
wait for her to join me and bring her gift

less like a homeless addict or crack-addled prostitute
taking in pills, powders, potions, the same ones
as frazzled housewives and supervisors
serving time in gray office cubicles

more like angels, we are telepathic self-medicators,
won't need to speak, as we offer and receive
with movements continuous, fluxing with light
or water, or blood, as the blessed forgetting begins.

WHAT IT IS TO GAMBLE

I lean from the wooden pew into smells
of deodorant stick, gin and limes, sea-wet wool
Pentecostal sensibility, my way of taking a chance
making one last throw, one call, one toss, one offering
deal me in, this high Whitsunday-staked wager
of white-robed newly baptized believers
I'm ready to gulp air aromatic with frankincense
snuffed candles, drink from the chalice, grapes
intoxicated in their own water sweetripe, fermented
chant Gregorian, be consecrated, be touched at the core
of my being, the final breaking of barriers
from which one never walks away the same

I'll risk it all to enter this rapture where all things stood once again
as they had before and what is left, what is not the exception
will resurrect, open its coffin, sit up slowly in such ritual
even atheists will cry out in celebration, in performance

I'm playing hard to claim a holy hole swallowing a divine hole
fire burning its own absolution inside of fire; the wind
at the core of the wind, the eye of God opening and closing
coming and going, opening and closing on me, sitting here
knowing what it is to gamble, and like any true crapshooter
knowing on the first roll of the dice, nothing is required of me
and then everything.

GIRL MOTHERING

I blow apart dandelion fluffs
scatter winged seeds over
primroses, marsh marigolds
things unsaid, undone between
my daughter and myself

a ewe approaches her lamb
that nibbles a half-curled frond
of fiddlehead fern into the shape
of an unknown alphabet's capital letter
found in a secret text on girl-mothering

words impossible to transcribe
shaped like the tender surrenders
I could have had with her, letting
her know she wasn't traveling alone
when she thought she was

how I should have stood guard
when the ravenous wolf who crouched
in her shadow lay lightly down and slept

a ewelamb spins and kicks
trots into and out of daughterhood
too fast, will probably be fed
and bedded, cared for, protected
a few more months
then slaughtered, butchered

the mother bred again, or sold as mutton

there is no absolution
nothing to forgive but time
and its disappearance

and nothing left
but dandelion puffs and
the scarlet fall of a lost ladybug
caught in a cowslip
trampled under hoof.

MELON

On your desk a jam jar of snapdragons and sweet peas
from my garden, my attempt at an apology
so far, we've gone deep enough into my melon disorder
borrowed nothing from anywhere else

I've already told you how it started when I was twelve and fat
and saw a picture of a model eating a cantaloupe
a goddess slicing into a green globe twined with beige rope
feeding herself a sliver of gold from a scraped, scarred old burlap ball

and decided to eat only melon for lunch
and breakfast and dinner

now, I tell you how I chop the honeydew into chunks
add a fourth of a cup of lime juice
very little sugar, some mint leaves, a blender
pour over ice, serve myself, weigh myself
then retch it all up; how it looks floating down there
bits of battered, smashed, flesh-colored meat
how the fetid odor of melons, tubers, bulbs
rises from the cold white toilet
floats around my naked kneeling form
up and out the white curtained window

next time, if there is to be a next time
I will tell you how someone might have done an awful thing to me
when I was twelve, but I can't tell you what, won't even whisper
those fat and dirty words

if you promise to do nothing during the whole of our hour
but bring yourself back; if each time you find yourself
drifting away you bring yourself back, if you stay with me
and my secret that can only be detected in the vomit

I will bring you more flowers.

WHERE WE HAVE BEEN

We called it a pond, but it's really a caught pool in a subdued stream
clusters of white bee boxes are still here, but half-opened water lilies
no longer curve up into porcelain cups balanced on flat indigo shadow-saucers

I did not miss it, it weighed nothing, didn't know it was a sin when I did it
didn't know while I was doing it, not even right after we had done it
but although I never forgot, I never memorized it, and later, much later
them telling me took me from you and any letting go to anyone else

for so many years I've pictured everything in my mind: your sensitive nose,
fingers that matched your quick and soft voice, how you arched your naked
back, how I lost the edges of myself in creeping unearthed roots, in you

nothing seems to be where it used to be; sweet smells of warmed, crushed seeds
are harder to distinguish now, buzzes and shakes of leaves are softer
almost a drowsy hum, some other things are not here either, frogs re-deeping
resonating their songs in the black sticky soil, the honeyed tenderness
of our raw, young rutting

jeweled damselflies dip over twig-bits circling lazily between harebells
of wild hyacinths that choke the pond of wiggleheaded polliwogs
I want to restore the place I've been trying to get to, want to recreate
the stories we told each other about each other, make the text of this place
fit what I've outlined, underlined, want to make ours once again
make it the *there* where we have been

I hold my hands in front of me like divining rods, they swing toward
fountains of sleeping sickness spewing over small drowned insects
that pockmark the surface that used to be a different place
I still believe that frogs lie dormant here, perhaps for years, under the mud
waiting for one perfect rainfall, temperature to spring them into rebirth

one large amber butterfly hangs thoughtfully from a reincarnated heatherbell
black marks on its wings like two eyes watch me question what I know although
there is no way to erase what I know, whenever I try, I sense something missing

a breeze scratches its back on a tree stump blackened beyond any future hope
of coming back to life, dead.

LACEMAKER

My grandmother told me
darning patterns on net
makes lace

all you need
is a single thread of floss
so fine you would think it was spun
by an albino weaving spider

a silver needle sharp and pure
as rubbing alcohol

a stolen porcelain thimble inlaid
with peridot crystals

the soft, hopeful light
of an amber enamel lamp

a cobalt glass goblet of
sweetened carbonated water
flavored with birch oil and sassafras

and of course you do need to submit
to the white, trembling
unanswerable logic
of making lace embroidery
on mosquito netting

it helps to have an armful of doves
lavender-necked, shy, quiet
fluttering gray brocade
wings on your roof

not to mention the moves
as practiced as a tango
of a good man who never leaves
scuff marks across your
newly polished wood floors.

WITHOUT ANY INTENTION

The willow drags
small sleeping swords
around the coherence of swans
breaking the surface
of the willow water
which replaces itself

even as a cygnet erupts
sloughing off stars
of lavender water
the pond resettles itself
back to white willow shadows
with ease

above my head
a thundering sound
of passing wings
their reflection
on the willow water
which the trumpeters
do not intend to cast
has no idea of its imposition

neither did you

I understand that now.

WE WAIT

In this seafront graveyard
where worm-kissed unbaptized babies
are buried, I continue to pretend to be
mostly satisfied with such arrangements
think of sacs and cauls, lace doilies
first communion and bridal veils
rose-carved ivory beads they will never know

yes, I'll wait for you here
where drizzle vinegars what is disguised
as a paralyzed dusk heavy with loss

wait until a stall of wind born in or of the sea
fills whatever is missing and there is nothing
left of any foretelling

I am reminded of baby orphans
who once dropped like awkward, newborn kids
into doe-steady hands; foster children,
the cold, skinny unwanted, growing up
placing their shoes and clothes under cots
in remodeled garages and back porches
hearing in the autistic sound of traffic
songs they learn to sing to each other
when they feel most alone and denied.

that's what women do, you see
walled up alive in our own bodies
when we wait, we think

especially here, close to ruins like this
washed in hyacinthine light
where late becomes early
and sea air combs sea grass
with rumors of salt
of light, of origin.

SPOKES OF A WHEEL

Coconut-oiled, under the straw beach umbrella
finally, the children have stopped fighting
and in dry cotton underpants, are asleep, head to head

spread out like hands on a clock, spokes of a wheel
or like rays they drew earlier with crayons
coming out from their yellow happy-faced suns
the pictures they argued over, pulled from each other

one tan body points north, but where I say tan I mean
sweat-oiled weight-lifter, and one pink body points west
and I mean a body for which a pink cheerleader bedroom awaits
one body so dark it seems painted-on and one so pale
it almost blends in with the glistening white sand

and holding their sea-salted dissension in our minds
like fingers against the revolving record of time
or prayers, because for so many of us
children are our way of praying

we watch the exposed positions of their flesh
change in conjunction with their dreams
and know they do not show direction
tell time or issue a rite of comfort

it is evident their separate bareness placed at arm's length
suggests a future ability to achieve loneliness

and the way each little fist is tightened around a crayon
speaks clearly of their impending and inevitable
tendency to jealously guard it, and even
in an unconscious state, to selfishly
hoard it.

COOL, DAMP PEACE

She has forbidden him to enter the backyard shed
that holds open shelves lined with rat poison
Mason jars of floating fruits, boxes of caustic lye

he comes here anyway whenever she starts to slosh vodka
into her early morning coffee, starts to screech
at him about his son-of-a-bitch father, his acne, God

he enters the holy and safe smells of moldering wood
enters his glue-sniffing euphoria

the problem with losing his mother
is that he keeps losing her again and again
it takes longer and longer for her to fall asleep
to stretch herself out on the kitchen counter
because she sees foul and leering snakes coupling on the floor

and he minds less and less, going for longer and longer
where, except for deadly nightshade that grows
through the slats and stings the air with its presence
the backyard shed holds cool, damp peace that banishes surprise
and a bittersweet, poisonous creeper
that crawls from the outside light
to suckle at the breast of the inside dark.

PEACH PIT

On the dirt road that circles the willowed pond, kids in cut-off shorts
sneak hits of pot, swig wine coolers, rub each other's slender bodies with oil
sunning their skins brown until they are all Spaniard, Jew, or Greek

behind barbecue pits, a burstly, young redhead with white, freckled skin
that does not tan, walks over to the circle of men squatting on coolers
passing whiskey and unfiltered cigarettes talking about their work
at the mills and slaughterhouses; she asks her daddy for a sip of his beer
fudge fat and belly hooting he yells at her to go join the kids, don't bother me

all her life she worried him like a puppy does a bone, wanted to know more
about the woman who was her mother, but he would make her pray
thank the good and almighty Lord that her mother strung together enough
sober days to go away and leave her with him
loved her enough to leave her

when these hollow feelings come near, she must act on them, fill them
goes to tables of fried onions, leftover fixings for hot dogs and hamburgers
her mother could have filled any emptiness, yet the emptiness she chose to fill
with enough love to leave it was this one, this girl who reaches into a bag of
fruit, brings out a peach, inhales its woody perfume, lets it nuzzle her hand
like a kitten's chin, then she lays her belly on the bench, longwise, alone in the
sun head hanging over the top, and she eats the peach
slurps it right down to the pit which she sucks then spits out

under the trees, young mothers, who know why they are, drone lullabies
in deep-song voices to bottle-sucking infants who look like their parents
the voices trail off, bodies sprawl on picnic blankets, murmurs, naps
the afternoon has become wide and quiet and she needs enough of it
to allow her to think many times over of the stranger she fancies within

she watches a glossy black bee settle on the peach pit, find a tiny bit of flesh
drink its nectar, drink, like the mother who loved her enough to leave her
loved her enough.

POTATO EYES

No need to shout my name, to repeat the call
in this house where, when anything warm boils
tears stream miraculously down insides of windows
before which I stand obediently stiff as was taught
look beyond him through lace living-room curtains
that hang in eternal limp and damp submission

he's drunk, repeats phrases from older monologues
I drop my chin, mumble obligation and duty talk
must peel the potatoes before Mother gets home
I explain softly, excuse myself, want to scream
to run away from his wretchedness, his flailing

as always, he reads my mind, damns the spuds to hell
orders me to sit down, now! prepares to retaliate
clenches a fist, crunches a tear down his face
jabs my aura with a cigarette, me loverly daw-haw-ter
who lazes and slops around, willna do as she's told

behind him foggy skies fall like silk parachutes
to be pierced on cathedral and church spires
I think crucifixes don't scrape heaven
they puncture it, I also think of my mother
how she explains his abandoned, betrayed soul
his love for us, I think of anything but his words
that claim me, disown me, praise me, curse me

then it's over and everything glass is weeping
except me, I'm not allowed sissified bawling
like the pot of ham and cabbage that boils away
as I set the table quietly, alert and listening
Monday night boxing is announced on television
tonight he'll eat dinner on a TV tray in there
it's really over, the blood-letting is at last
over, and this time, I feel less than last time
except for the sting of duty and perhaps relief
that there are potatoes waiting to be peeled.

HE WANTS TO LET HIMSELF GO

She shows him how to throw down enough frozen peas
for the stoplight parrotfish and yellowtail snappers
to swim between his legs and nibble
when he goes too far she pulls him inland
wants him to walk heavily, steadfastly
afraid of the ledge

but he likes the overhanging face of rock
walks to it dangling one foot over the abyss
likes the rush of adrenaline when he almost falls
loves to catch himself at the very last second
feels alive, feels light, wants one day to drop
from the coral-cliff edge to the bottom
where lobsters crawl in and out of small holes
to the bluing rhythm of giant sea-turtle shadows

wants to go where the green moray eel goes
remain still and quiet when the big stingray
slides straight to and over his face
and slurps through his hair in its squid search
he wants to let himself go until he thinks he is drowning
but isn't

she has told him how the mystic swims
in the same waters in which the psychotic drowns
but he knows more, knows that when he can reach the eel
it will offer itself like a rescue rope

she doesn't tell him the rest, how she will either die or go mad
when he goes so deep, deeper than deep, enough
until he can see it is not an eel, nor a rope
offered by her to reel him back up, but a hand
hanging weightless in the warm water
there for him to do whatever he asks, a hand
that eventually he will recognize
as his own.

CALLIOPE

That young woman with a red barrette
clipped to frizzled yellow hair
rides the merry-go-round
every Wednesday when it rains

she mounts a red-yellow porpoise
insolently refuses to hold on
grumbles like a drunken sailor
at alternating red and yellow lights
blurred into a herd of haloes

identifies nameless brushstrokes
that run and bleed
into scarlet floating beasts
on painted, golden seas

doesn't think it a bit odd
to go around and around
to a tape-recorded calliope
in the pouring mid-morning
of a darkening high-school day

smiles an ardent satisfaction
shows all the wires on her teeth
to the carousel operator
who gives her another free ride

he lights a cigarette, pulls the handle
waits again as she color crayons her world
fills in yellow and red, red and yellow
between all the cool-lit, fine lines of rain.

THIS ONE HIT, THIS SNIFF

Barrio, motherless, ghetto boy
who can't read or write, spray-paints
blobs in red, on rusted canisters
in the chemical dump, snorts the can
kicks at an invisible junkyard dog
with metal-tipped boot; sniffs
his own sour armpits. Fleas,
sated and half-sated bloodsuckers
dance to the fluting of gnats.
He joins them, postures as if on stage,
scratches an invisible guitar.

The green-grubbed sunshine
evaporates the half-eaten night,
burns off fog, exhales odors for him
to inhale in his search
for glue, turpentine, cleaning solvents.

Street boy, who belongs to no one,
snuffs up stench of rotten garlic,
fermenting meat, coffee grinds,
skins of molting roaches,
plucks a bit of fennel that sprouts
between the fence that keeps nettles,
flesh-eating black flies & mosquitoes
neither in nor out; rips the plant apart
shoves the tough scented weed
under his nose, this wild fennel,
anise heated up to licorice.

His childhood was planted with bulbous fennel,
baby-green feathers curled up in fronds,
a scent that could drown him in yesterday
if he let it, he prays to whatever listens:
*Okay, give it to me, mainline me
save me, yes, give me this now, just this one
hit, this sniff, this fragrant zone that
smells, smells, smells like licorice
and being wanted, wanted, wanted by someone.*

FISH DON'T MOURN

Two goldfish the same peach of painted blossoms
on porcelain, one floats upside down, languishes on a bottom
fossil-rock, sighs watery messages, I tap the fish tank
when you care about something you want it to care back
look at this, I call my friends, they shake their heads
something is terribly wrong with that fish, then it dies

I wrap it in white facial tissues, bury it in a terra-cotta pot
of marigolds, next to the window by the fish tank
everything will still be the same, only a little different
I tell the other fish who swims over, sends me lonely fish
thoughts, spreads bridal-veil tail and fins in a surrender
to a sad, sad water dance, poor thing misses its mate
says my mother, whose husband wasted stubbornly
in their broken yellow kitchen for twenty years, she
bending beside him to listen only to his rage, which finally
mercifully, floated off in a whiskey veil of veined shimmer

little fish don't mourn, say the people at the pet shop
trying to sell aquarium remedies, it's sick, that's all
I'm just looking, thank you, browsing, passing through
feverish, I've arrived, later, I will leave, cool

I find it, the color of moonlight on daffodils, buy it
pour it in, sit down with my mother, watch them avoid
each other, chase each other, nibble the bubbles between them
charge their blood with recycled oxygen, swim swimmingly
through dancing shards of long, quiet light

see how gradually the inconsolable is consoled, speak the words
to my mother, let them roll in my mouth, write them down
like how newly courageous they look on the page, write it all down
and the point, the lesson I've compacted here

is that when it comes to loneliness
there is little difference between missing your mate
after tending him for twenty years, any mourning
and all little goldfish thoughts.

VISITING DAY

She waits properly for the bus, ladylike
to bring her son bitter chocolates, sweet oranges
is calmly prepared for a late or early arrival

stands straight, careful not to lounge like street prostitute
or fast food server outside sneaking a smoke
assumes the suitable stance of one who waits

properly at the correct spot, she taught him
his little hand in hers, what was proper, did her best
but doesn't forget the only perfect parent
created two children who disobeyed
oh yes, there are always influences
Adam accused Eve, Eve accused the serpent

she waits with fare in hand, glances down the street
checks her watch, presses the coins into her palm
tastes a metallic tang in the back of her throat, sour
like staggered time, like thoughts of a young man
stabbing another, enough to kill him, knowing
we electrocute men who make unforgivable mistakes
electroshock those who make lesser ones

she does not look, nor does she close her eyes
to shut out the righteous man across the street
who staple-guns flyers onto telephone poles
tucks them properly under windshield wipers
calls out harsh language burned into words
warns everyone to get saved, the end is near

this is a distraction, an influence that keeps her sane
holds back the fear that there may be blame inside her
simply waiting to rise all around her, choke her with herself

a great energy of deliverance moves towards her
a charcoal bus of sketched visitors on a round-trip ride

the air, thick as the breath of condemned men, shudders
the door opens, she enters the redeeming vignette.

SHE TAKES OFF HER CLOTHES

The slick magazine photographer who is knocked out by her beauty
wants to do the shoot in her living room, wants her to take off her clothes
a little at a time, places her between the huge, black carving of Shiva Shakti
and the emerald and lapis ceramic elephant chair from India

she takes off her clothes for lights and reflectors
poses on overstuffed furniture, curls under gold-tasseled paisley scarves
under a picture of Jesus with raw, bleeding heart hanging outside his chest
and blood running down his face from a thorned wreath stuck in his forehead

she takes off her clothes for Hollywood, New York and *Playboy*
next to a shrine to a Buddha who exposes a naked, fat tummy for all to rub
and smiles without coughing or wrinkling his nose at the smoke
from the dry ice that burns in the abalone shell

she takes off her clothes for the warm, moist pleasure of pleasing
the photographer who licks his lips and moves around her and begs her
begs her to spread her breasts and thighs a little more, yes, like that, more

she takes off her clothes, and suddenly nothing is holy and everything is holy
and one day she'll understand why and it will make perfect sense
it will be all right and she won't even need to ask forgiveness.

PART TWO

MUSCLE AND SLUR

Suicidally beautiful young men
of undeniable inner virtue
drink Jack and Coke to get warm
soak themselves in pomposity
in spite of being dressed in asthma
pimpled necks, nervous blinking

fragrant with fear, wishes, they march off
to bunker fortifications of quartz, mica
granite promises of courage under fire
the muscle and slur of a belief in some kind
of daring outpost of foreign warmth

you have seen for yourself haven't you
when they come home, relieved of the freight
of brotherhood, bravery, tired of being strong
how they become ill, stressed with post trauma
feel guilty for being sick, used up

become lifeless ghosts of young men
papery shadows of form, so understated
they are merely brooding memories of form

become a concussion of winter-spiced
stinging snowfalls exquisite in soft impressions
of their gentle selves

turned into uninvited white stallions
standing still, lost, herdless under shelterless
leafless, black breaking branches.

RAGA

He tells her he wants a new feeling, wants to force the lotus open

a peacock fans his tail, performs a mating dance
for what he has always believed to be some dull, sad peahen

she inserts a newly recorded raga cassette into the tape player
anxiously offers him sugarcane juice over ice

from the grove, a discontented green cloud of parakeets rises
he says there must be some cohesiveness, some tonal system
calls for turning up the volume

microtones break down across the grass below the verandah
clambering monkeys shake one red blossom from one flame tree
he explains conventions, starting points, ending formulas

sips more sugarcane juice over ice and it makes him think
he can taste rain-white jasmine, cool as the last ice cube
rhythmic patterns in the unvaried melody
fall and roll into one faint pink streak of evening
and he's getting a new feeling

the feeling he wanted, he's getting it
improvised, not broken in, this variation on the traditional

it's raw and impure like a bamboo-hidden insect at the edge of passion
breathless, enough to make him thick-speeched, chirping

she releases, knows now he will not send her away, not this time
not as long as she loves him enough to keep inserting variations
within a prescribed framework

she smiles benignly, averts her eyes, agrees with him how
it is truly beautiful the way light flows between two identical dark edges

how tiny flames cause the river over there to flicker as if catching fire
as hundreds of clay lamps float together, downstream.

MAN WITH A BIRTHMARK

Unthinkingly, as a dog might look
upon hearing someone speak its name
the man with a birthmark like Gorbachev's
tips over his shopping cart
in the alley behind the office building
behind the approaching uniform

he turns his head to her, it's a simple human need
this need to sleep

the security guard is a big, beautiful woman
with brown-black puppy eyes
she orders him to the shelter
where the homeless are warm and happy
warns him away, uses no weapons, just words

air passes through shapes of openings as he tries to speak
she inhales the designs of his attempts, doesn't care
has made a career of being unimpressed

he tries to explain that he is thick tongued, gives her poems
tries to carve out a core of a mind
she is, of course, startled, but they are not poems
they are packing slips, invoices, gas receipts
although well-written not about anything that matters

it begins to rain, drops that do not get heavy
but fall sullenly and are eked from the sky
she tears his scraps of paper, rips apart his webs of words
the spaces between them, she is uninterested
in the mentally disordered, his birthmark
that darkens and ripples as he breathes in
too much dripping air, and before her astounded eyes
he drowns.

SCATTERING

Somewhere between Alcatraz and Angel Island
we tip and pass the urn, leaded pottery is heavy
and I'm feeling a bit queasy on this rough sea
scattering ashes, what drunken poet called them ashes?
gravel and gray bits of bone pour like coarse stones
into the wet, darkening maw and I hate being here
as much as I hate hating him, don't want to blame
try to get the god thing together, though no god ever cared
one way or the other about my theology

I pray anyway that I won't show my streak of meanness
like those others who didn't like him much either
and grope to transform excuses into kind comments
squawking gulls bicker back at the human chattering
and in a spectacular display of sanctifying grace
they peck and burst the blessed sky with honest beaks

I lift my face, try to catch the rain in my wrinkles
so it looks like tears, feels like tears, turns into tears

a singular gull floats close by as I hurriedly lean out
spill my guts over his ashes, a chunk of my vomit
a piece of his bone, froth, what's the difference?
—something catches in her oval white downy breast
there is an indignant screech, a flash of wings
a spewing of the authentic, a dangle of scrawny legs
an exceptionally strange and radiant gift of rainlight
hope, getting on with it, and she's gone.

MAN WITH EASTER ISLAND HEAD

The large man with the Easter Island head
all chiseled brows and nose, moves around the shelter
like a domesticated ox, black, with thick, sad gestures
carries his wound everywhere with him
like an empty flask needing to be filled with water
he can't find his mother, his little brother
his home, even his street is underwater

asks everyone who looks like a doctor or nurse
but no matter how hard he tries, he cannot describe
his skinless, bloodless wound, cannot show it
measure it, identify it, or himself, just knows
it is killing him and there's no ice in the morgue
no morgue, not even sheets to cover the dead

he makes a fist, beats at his chest, tries to punch
his pain dead center, sorry, someone says
you are not the only one who has lost everything
who is alone and lost with nowhere to go
but for now you need to move on, get along
keep going

he refuses to go nowhere, refuses to do
what he's told, stops, digs in
people pass around him; he closes his eyes
feels himself begin to sink back into a kind of return
lets himself sink through sewage, gasoline, putrid currents
of stink and decay, sink down into the wet land
deeper than the ooze of carcasses

lets himself sink and sink through the minutes
the years to come until only his colossal head remains
to be, like he saw on the television documentary
one mysterious, anonymous ancient remain
of unknown origin.

ASH TUESDAY

I think I recognize you
trudging across my television screen
dazed, like all the other downtown refugees
bouncing off the terror of not one, but two
planes exploding into skyscrapers

I think it is you, heading for the bridge
beard and brows grayed from where ashes two feet deep
fly about like little dirty snowflakes

It might be your voice they report being heard
calling for help on the cell phone buried
beneath tons of concrete rubble
it might be your body, burning, leaping
hand in hand with another, into the air
a thousand feet up

fists to my eyes, I phone, but can't get through
I e-mail your colleagues, your old girlfriend
but no one knows where you are
or who else might be able to reach you

so, falling back into the safety of the rest of us
I turn to whoever I care about is closest
and say hey, I always meant to tell you: I love you
—only to find that same person turning
to do the same to another and another turning to do
the same to me, don't worry, we say earnestly
with valiant intent, we shall overcome

and I am stirred with the stoutheartedness
of all of us; the goodness of our grand reaching
our veins pierced to donate blood
our workers staunchly rescuing, rallying
oh beloved masses, oh fine and intent people
oh nation of hands outstretched and offering
hey, I always meant to tell you:
I love you.

DEPARTURE

Airplanes trail grisly white contrails
that quickly stitch themselves with gashes

the lines, the runways, the lies
that kept my home in its place
have dissipated; can't pencil them back in

in the aftermath of dread
I have arrived at this act of departure
that is no longer paralyzed
by fluorescence

I thought I had written completely
all I had to give as a passenger
up until now, and if I receive
anything true in return, I will smuggle it

through whirs of ventilation, reheated
sweat, security scanners, metal detectors

carry it inside my head as felt-tipped pen
permanent black ink

in the bunker-tight airport
I will outline a new window
on an existing wall that is all windows

one that no indifferent window cleaner or
weary security checker can spray-wipe clean

a space to set free this port of air

once again reclaimed by air travelers
clear enough to let in at least one amethyst night
filled with copper clouds

and safe enough for preflighters
to view the majesty of benign take-offs
water dripping from silver wings
in showers of opals.

AS LONG AS IS NECESSARY

We extinguish yellow lamps, pour brandy in coffee
try to talk just loud enough to hear ourselves over
the soft snores of our children asleep in the campsite

the subject and object of our litany is divorce, how we
care too much about each other to continue like this
the awful acts that got by because the words were right
what went awry, amiss, why we must not continue

we hug, you smell of insect repellent and sand
it feels as if you might have started crying
I keep holding you because when I pull back from the hug
you will see that I'm not crying like you, you think I am
but I'm not, this is simply a hug lasting only as long as is necessary
and it kills me from the bottom up, I want you to think
that it's under control even though I am on the brink
of nothing I can honestly name, no one's to blame

kerosene fumes vaporize, the night continues to speak in tongues
above our heads, chitters and snaps and cracklings clamor the syllables
of the disappointment we feel, and all around us on rustling leaves
padded feet scamper and spread more syllables of all the love
we silently, earnestly, sympathetically intend, the love, oh
the love that sustains, has sustained, will sustain, we pray
to whatever god will listen, for as long as is necessary.

WHARF WITHOUT PURPOSE

I refuse to lunch at that simple little unnamed three-table place
identified only by an "elf service" sign; the "s" has fallen away
no one has bothered to put it back, instead I pluck a can of beer
from mounds of manufactured snow while you buy fifty cents' worth
of seal food to toss at the sea lions that bark and splash in the oily water

I don't want to do what you want to do anymore, won't compromise
feel guilty, selfish, don't care, care, offer to share the beer in an act of giving
toss my own pennies when the organ grinder's monkey begs for coins
but the enthusiasm keeps leaving me, it evaporates there on the wharf
into the glistening cold sea-air, even the monkey retreats from my deficiency,
won't even reward my donation with a peck on the cheek, but you do
oblivious to the sense of something falling away, the inability to put it back

I am less than I was before, squid and red snappers stare openmouthed
as if startled at the sight of me and the initiative that flees from me
I become sentimental, want to treat you with unusual gentleness
we buy walk-away crab cocktails, sit on a bench of worn planks
attached lovers crazily and drunkenly pass like we used to
you think we still do, but the "s" has fallen from the self, I am elf
serving up the last scrapings of affection, no sense in telling you it's gone
suddenly, having lost it, more than willing now to deem it fondness

the sky fades to gray, the sea creases into a sheet of aluminum
we watch tourists emerge like noisy frogs after the rain
they migrate comfortably across the wharf without purpose
we continue to sit, list together and apart, shift, shudder, grow slack
I politely let you take my hand and as the afternoon begins to fracture
a banshee takes up silent keening at the final loss of her long dying elf.

AROUND YOU

When I first met you
from a knotted plastic bag
where it swam honey-silken
around and around, as if
expecting the water to simply
go on and on, you swallowed the goldfish
stopped my startled heart
then regurgitated it back
like it was a hunk of peeled apricot

when you spit it into a glass bowl of water
where the poor little creature
swam around and around
in the same, but not the same, circle
I was yours, yes, I said, to all you asked

today, not for the first time since your diagnosis
I don't intervene as you threaten, this time
to smash the bulbs and chew the glass
as you struggle to unwrap and lay out
the tangled Christmas tree lights

you rage at how stupidly I put them away
in a sloppy hurry, knotting them around themselves
purposefully, to make you struggle like this

I run from the room and you think
it is because of my guilt

but it is how, before you began blaming
I caught a glance of myself
in the mirror over the sofa
and I reeled back at the vision
of me all gold and light
going around and around you
on and on, around you, swimmingly.

SOMETHING VERY UNCOMFORTABLE

I want an apology, a slightly wet regret, sorrow
you give sword lily flowers

I have no vase large enough
so you overturn my tall, fat tin of licorice sticks
empty them all out
squeeze fat stemmed gladioli
into the unresisting open-mouth

you don't fill it with water

and this time I don't follow after you
doing what you can't be bothered with

gobs of pink-orange and red-yellow
prevail on my counter, to glance at
passing by, a glance of flush
the way a face does, and the life inside it
after a slap

something very uncomfortable
about the way they wilt
the way you throw them, plop
into soggy tea leaves and ashes

I should have given them water

hold myself responsible
especially for the lower, unopened buds
who don't have a chance
no matter how hard they try
to burst themselves open
they have to go too

beg no one's pardon, make up my mind
do what I have decided to do
wash the tin in sterilizing suds
ask where you have put the licorice sticks
you said you left them where they fell
on the windowsill, exposed to the heat of the sun
and they dried out

it's my fault, I could have picked them up
sealed them in moisture-proof wrapping

something very uncomfortable
going on here and it is not a flutter
but a series of chains, tugging like linked tethers.

A CERTAIN PINK CRY

He says he isn't going to hit her
not now, not ever again   it shames him
each memory of each last slap

but the way he is holding the keys
                    the way he moves toward her. . .
she backs away, bumps into the kitchen table

he hates it when she backs away
throws the keys, they fall cluttering at her feet
she does not pick them up, does not move
looks where he points,
                    a gray clump of hair
with too many quivering parts climbs down the table leg

probably came in on the tropical fruit
he says, as if it's her fault,
                    when it comes to spiders
he has taught her the right thing to do, swiftly
no time for astonishment, no time for pity

with the brown inside of an empty cardboard box
she lifts and drops her arms, up and down, up and down
even as its terrified legs reach out, she doesn't stop
until she has smashed the little creature, beaten it to death

once, when her father holstered it from the ceiling
of the butcher shop and gashed and slit its pink throat
the pig let out a high squeal of a scream

that same cry now pierces her eardrums
she doesn't know from what mouth it comes

only knows a certain pink cry of tongue
of inner ear, of creature, of flesh
not human, perhaps of pork
freshly skinned

cries out.

DOVE MEAT

My mother-in-law drops pasta
into salted steam, cries in Italian
"Why do you do this to me?"

I add bitters, more cherry juice
to her vermouth and whiskey
the way she likes her Manhattans
the way she taught me to like them
I like them, I like her
I don't like her son anymore.

She talks about the dove meat
in this special Adriatic gravy
the last one warbled "I'm sorry"
and she said "I don't mean it"
going ahead, slicing its throat
so the blood spurted cleanly.

She calls her husband, pauses sadly
calls mine, gestures to the bottle, to me
wants me to pour the garnet-flushed wine
wants to shame our marriage back together

I do not pour, instead I quietly spoon sauce
over the pasta where between red clots
eyes of small birds blink up at me.

It's over, there are no more options
dinner is served, the men enter
sit down, ignore the flashing red lights
the empty wine glasses, my screaming silence.
It is time for dinner. We eat.

GRANDMOTHER SPIDER

We sit in her serious kitchen of cobalt tile
the blue of her beloved Evening in Paris bottles
she sets out retsina, feta, pomegranates
a jar of roasted red peppers, slices of sausage

if you must stay with him, she tells me
remember in the void between the strands, the air is airier

what you weave must be languid, silken, dusky
must blow in light and shifting gusts
the more connected you are to him
the more serious the possible shrinkage

always keep your mouth shut with a drunk
you can never win, not even break even

let him pretend to be more than part of a road crew
that replaces sewage pipes, when others ask him
what he does, he will expect you to distract them
do right angles and triangles, little geometric puzzles

the moment he realizes that those he doesn't like
don't like him back, pull prayers from boxes
wear the face of one who works behind airline counters

if you must stay with him remember
the air carries the silence, the tenant controls the landlord
the slave, the owner

the weaver of the web
holds all the tension.

NEWLY DIVORCED

Sometimes there is a man
untypecast, sleeping curled beside her

before he leaves, she will learn him
the humiliated waiter, the swamper
the fired bowling alley bartender

find herself still wanting
wonder if she doesn't hate him yet
how soon will she

however strangely she exists
fantasies breeding and rebreeding
she carries on, playing the woman

sadly, too young to be seasoned
too divorced to be equal.

NOT MY UMBRELLA

I think I left my umbrella at that Irish bar last night
black with a small rip, silver shaft, cracked black handle
didn't bring it home; brought him home though
out of his mind with drink, singing, spouting Celtic poetry
just for tonight I told him as they escorted us from the pub
and I want you gone by morning, I issued my prerequisite
spending a ridiculous amount of time giggling
looking for the key, then for the lock

this morning's weather report calls for rain

the bartender empties out the lost-and-found cardboard box
some eyeglasses, one gray woolen glove, three lighters
there is one black umbrella but it isn't mine
I hesitate, want to be honest, this one is unripped
silver dragon handle, newer, more expensive
for the love of god, woman, he says, take the damn thing
winking, gold freckles in his green eyes

I grab the umbrella, claim the damn thing that is not mine
the other umbrella hadn't been mine either
nor the one before that, nor you, still sleeping in my bed
probably waiting for my return and breakfast
another damn Irishman, each time I lose one of you
another tribesman turns up in your place
like something being returned
not quite what was lost, but once again mine

I step outside into the continuance of my hangover
the newness of rain; umbrellas open all around me
reflect the darkening sky, wild-black morning glories
hang upside down from thousands of silvered threads.

HACKER

He's in my living room, hunched over
his laptop, today he wears camouflage sagging pants
that currently constitute teenage chic reminiscent of prisons
where inmates are prohibited from wearing belts

says with the easy voice of someone who medicates
his own life; society does not own me like it does you

hackers are feared for all we know about computers
but our real power is in how well we know you

like how you all choose your passwords poorly
routinely pick access codes like "sesame"
or your favorite hobby, or your own name
you want me to penetrate, want me

you can convince any computer of any lie
give it the incorrect information correctly and it will believe

he goes back to tapping on his keyboard
long conversations with people in various time zones
in virtual spaces; hacks away, drifts away on winged feet
into cyberspace only to encounter adoring messages
from men and women who claim to be young girls

come here, babe, he types the words beautiful in their insolence
let me do you . . like you . . like to be done

in the looseness of his snail-blue gaze
I anxiously wonder if sooner or later I will give in, cross over
and be doing it with him, for him, to him

his mouth slowly working the air, relax, he whispers
pulling me to his power, his sex in my e-mail
putting his fingers over mine on the keyboard

it's already started; it's happening
now.

LOST LOT OF US

All of us, we long for a form
iced and pre-dawn, perhaps a unicorn
anything forgotten, colorless
that snorts and stamps quietly
but with thunder
we present eyes and throats
to mother-of-pearl hooves
offer marshmallowy lips to white jade tongues
in cut-crystal mouths, surgically cured
do it, we call, delirious, we beg, do it
all of us rise, sniff, reach in surrender
toward eternal, ever falling snow
like love, without thawing time
past blood-smeared mists
into a nether land of
more of us, the whole lost lot of us
all of us, fevered, yearning
to receive the pure sword of sanction
into our primal ooze of sin
aching for the cold silvered touch
of the beast
—the shock.

HE MUST LIKE PRISON

It's like a drug, this attraction to you
I can't will it away, can't even will away
the will to try; I'm much too eager
reaching for you, the guards look offwards
how many times have I suggested
if we were married, we could have conjugal rights

I have sent you chocolate, blue jeans that fit
peanuts, potato chips, stamps and paper
so that you can write me back, drive all night
to visit you, bring your mother, your sister, money
he must like prison, they say, he keeps going back

you are beautiful in tan muscles, blond everywhere
when loving me, which, when you could
you never did as much as I wanted

what about the boys in there with you, their fingers
buttocks, tongues, what about sex, I want to know
how can you ask me to wait for you
you answer my question with a question
apologize for your anger

by the way, that photo of me I sent, you frown
it worries you to see me looking so tired
trying too hard to appear happy
to tell the truth
I thought it was one of my best
wonder what fellow inmate
it was supposed to impress

you begin to quote the Bible to me
oh sweet Jesus, you are so gorgeous
so impossible, so dogmatic

nothing specifically has changed
although suddenly I'm sensible

you are more beautiful than you will ever know
and I'm leaving.

HUG

I jump, collide with you and you
lean into me like a ski jumper
stomach to stomach, heart to heart
holding, slightly rocking side to side

like people in Chagall paintings
floating just off the ground
toes pointing in odd directions
we soar free of ties and ropes
lift through ourselves balloon light

a bottomless green-blackness tingles
in the upper air; the empty sky
flies into pieces, the present moment
ten thousand white-crowned sparrows

trees collect wings, the gull beaks
of unopened magnolias strain upward
as if pulled by strings, leaves
become promises of us, together again
promises that send us reeling apart
drunk, deaf, breathless
trembling as if we had just been fighting

we turn from each other
hold hands, take a step forward

and the world is made flat
once again.

PART THREE

SHE KISSES STEAM

Though she can no longer live alone
no matter where my mother lives now
she will always be alone, pouring late afternoon
into Aunt Minny's heirloom porcelain cups
to be taken poshly with one milk, two sugars
carefully passed on hand-painted saucers
of pink English roses, edged with gold

in the back garden of the home for the elderly
we sit on a bench, sip water from Styrofoam cups
we converse, the way ladies do, chat about
those fat brown birds who shout at one another
their songs drowning in heaps and heaps of peony petals
watch a bee climb inside a fuchsia and fly back out
talk without hurry about hollyhock and foxglove
the refined young lady I am indeed becoming

she enters this secret garden where insects and birds sleep
with hands folded, her memories, velvet butterfly heads
powder themselves with pollengold blessings
little girl imaginings, enchanted stories
forever lovely now in her mind, she tells me again
what a lovely young lady I am becoming, doesn't see
this aging mother of a mother, leathery jowls, crow's feet
sees only loveliness, lifts her face dreamily, languidly
and each wrinkle reforms into tiny etched flowers and stars
around her happily brimming eyes

I don't worry about her brain, I cherish her soul
which turns to fairy tales and songs, and I go there
into them, with her, oh mother, I am here, you are safe
I love you; each time I leave her there are no good-byes
instead she concentrates on her cup of tea, purses lips
lowers eyelids, begins to hum a hushed and soft lullaby
good night, sleep tight, she tucks it away for later
and sips her water as though lovingly, thoughtfully
she kisses steam from freshly brewed tea.

CONVALESCENT CONVERSATION

White and starched, she bends, sniffs petals
tilts her head at him, raises a brow

I'm not too old yet to smell, he growls,
to recognize the stench of slime and shit

daisies are not perfumed, she singsongs,
their scent is raw, green fed

(her tongue squirms out the words
like a creature probing out of scum)

like the insides of fresh eggs
caught suddenly on stems, she goes on
pretty in a farm-field way
don't you think?

I don't think of stinking daisies
but of displaced chocolates

(she had emptied out semi-sweet chunks
for damned putrid weeds)

the chocolates she tosses on his tray
look like they've finally had it

nothing has died, she smile-spits,
that we cannot do without

everything she touches, he thinks,
would be better off left alone

everything? she asks.

YOUR OLD HOUSEFLY

You sell roasted chestnuts to tourists in sequined pillbox hats
meet other old men, every day, worn but still vending
in shadows of mosque domes and minarets, joke about me
say you will take a younger wife, call me your old housefly
is this what I have waited for all these years?

here, behind shut gates and decomposing walls, is your old housefly
more eager than any young wife could ever be, still indulging
still polishing your jeweled pistol handles and gold water pipes

look, my wings are perfect, there is metallic green on my body
and my strings of legs can still walk about you in a slow curved dance
like those of a bride just dismounted from camel or ox
before I become clumsy with the burden of myself
take me into your mouth, swallow me, be gorged and satiated
forage, old man, bury your face into my putrescence
my ferment and bubble

on silk scarves I set out pistachios, apple tea, myself
am ripe for plunder, my lifelong love, drink
from this heavy, bloated carcass, extract a precious drop
of the fecundity of me, draw it into your limp soul
stir it to life again, swallow from this heap of me

a young wife, hah! she won't know how to dip into your body
and pull out the date pits of pain lodged in your back
her gristly thighs, clamping for a son you cannot make, will kill you
but don't worry, you won't die alone, her family will close in
whispering how you are so old, you are already rotting in your grave

and you will be wretched, looking out of the window, waiting for me
crying out for your old wife, mother of your daughters, your love
but I will have become what you have made me, hanging from the ceiling
fast asleep, dreaming of filigreed palaces and fat painted elephants
and the fecal feast that falls for me from under their raised, quivering tails.

SHINE OF MY OWN RELIEF

I stand at the screen door
watch my husband drag out the rowboat
the old, ripped, life jacket, the one rotten oar
and I gag on my worry
will hold it there all day

he has set the borders of the jigsaw puzzle
leaving the rest for me to fill in
but I tip over the card table, will not finish his puzzle

there will be enough time later
for whatever is left of whoever survives
to complete the final picture

I walk my backyard hill that overgrows
with wild fuchsia, blackberry creepers
dense snarls of our lives, jeweled insects
that sing in syllables, forecast how, in the end
one of us will bury the other

the mature tree I once wrapped as a sapling
in burlap and chicken wire has lost its leaves
it trembles its age through its trunk, scratches
with its stripped branches on hoary clouds
black runes that translate how
there is no quick way to loosen the tie between us
it must be set free in increments

a voice calls my name, he waves from the boat
laughs, holds up a fish, I actually see
in the sheen of the lake
the shine of my own relief, feel a sharp thrill

the entire moment becomes silver lit
astonishingly alive, silhouetted
against a darkening, navy-blue sky

then released.

OVERNIGHT IN THE LIGHTHOUSE

The interior has long, curved staircases
with smoothly polished brass banisters, I go up one flight
wait for the trailing part of my life
to catch up with me, do not look for direction
have what I can manage, need only to work with transitions
I didn't want to know, I told her, no I didn't
I really didn't want to know what she told me

go up another flight of this rented lighthouse
to an octagonal bedroom of angles and sides
where her suicide leans in on me, syllable by syllable
she was a story for a slow, patient, careful reader
one that was sighed out, I know things about you
I said, damning her to a future when she would always be
the person who would need the other person most

I can't stay in the motel with the mourning family
need to pull myself out from under my compliance
with their pretending it was an accident

but everything here is lit from within by a torch
that was lit from another and another before that
and another, a force field that exists
as a purpose for the paying out of lies

I wash my hair and bathe, put on flannel nightclothes
because there must be another night
and a better reason than that of a warning
why the brightest light in the lighthouse
must always shine away from the center.

WILD SUGAR

Of course I remember you, and your birthday, between
the buck and warp of language, we begin to recall markers
it was a dress-up party, mind your manners, folding chairs
tied with bubble-gum pink balloons on freshly mowed thick lawn
tables with real linen tablecloths, set for little-girl-tea

your mother rented a machine to whip colored spun sugar
we took turns, gathered it all up, wound it around paper cone holders
you called it cotton candy, fairy floss, but to me it was wild sugar

your hair hung in real curls, honey brown silk, blue satin bow
mine was frizzy home-permed, the color of rotting hay

neither could say what the matter was because we didn't know
what we meant was please, please like me

you were a chiffon-frothed blue butterfly fluttering at me like a pulse
I whirled you around an inflorescence of crushed daisies
don't know how you put up with my second-hand horror of a frock
twirling you around and around in a needy, clumsy dance

nonsense, you say, until then you had been so very lonely
wandering alone through bruised hollyhock and wilted dahlia
never forgot that party, us, dancing all curly and green in the light

spinning and giggling at how I insisted on calling it wild sugar
pink shreds of sugar clouds sticking silverly to our fingers

it was grand, how you asked me to stay after the rest left
said I could eat as much wild sugar as I wanted

all that bribing; how could we have possibly known
the perfect floating circle of ourselves we were

and here we are, returning to the small satisfactions
talking, taking the soul's way of laying down comfort
refilling the other's little-girl teacup
with sweet grown-up kindness
pouring ourselves out with what could have been, but was not
and purposefully, delicately, drinking of it.

BOUGAINVILLEA

Even though I await his visits, it's so difficult
to stifle yawns and at the same time pretend to listen
politely to the preaching he calls conversation

he comes on Sunday afternoons to sit with us
in the garden and he is so young, so beautiful
I'm willing to spend time with him, even forgive
his earnest attempts to save my immortal soul

try not to stare too intently at his eyelashes
lowering like insect feathers on his peach cheeks
his languishing slenderness, his exquisite sensuality

try to focus on the other old patients who in turn
stare mindlessly at the whooshes of water sprinklers
that spin around their own rainbowed lenses
splash the magenta bougainvillea leaves
which look like, but are not, flowers

the young priest frowns his sincerity, offers salvation
warns if I don't believe in his god, then I must
alternatively believe in another god, or in no god, or
the reverse of god, or many gods, or what looks like
but isn't the death of god, begs me to believe in something

well I do, I believe I would love a stiff gin and tonic
or two, to help me settle into a sun-warmed, gentle sleep
hold back the pain of these crippled fingers, these bones
that grow inside like wooded vines, drying, shrinking

I close my eyes, pretend to nod off, fake a bit of a snore
until satisfied he's said all he can, he rises
to cross the lawn to hear another joyless confession
before leaving behind his lingering words

thinking them hummingbirds, dragonflies, midges
blessings, prayers that might feed at fuchsia blooms
not knowing they are only bribes, momentary lovelies
that snag themselves like spurious petals
on sharply hooked, wet thorns.

WALTZ

". . . and after the snowflakes,"
she whispered, "believe it or not,
the flowers are going to waltz"

tip-toeing beyond neatly trimmed lakes
no edges, no horizon, just backdrops
theatrical in flowered bushes
they arched prettily into spotlights
flushed with rose and lilac

outside, in the shadow of Macy's
in drizzle, on a dirty brown blanket
a woman sits like a crippled ballerina
holding cardboard that reads "hard times"
not allowed a corner for fixing broken things
some dreamy Sunday afternoon
while sunbeams, saffron with fairy dust
enter open windows on air that smells faintly
of rose and lilac flowers in the garden
waiting their turn to waltz

how did it ever come to this?
I asked that part of me that always knows
right there, in the theater
and the way, as usual, was shown—
the dance finished and the exit
as indicated, was through the entrance.

HER GOOD HEARTH

Sometimes, there are no matches
in her humble household

if she fails to keep the fire alive
she explains, coming to my kitchen
she can do no cooking

she must go to the house of a neighbor
and ask for some fire

this is why, then
with rice husks in the fireplace
her fire is always kept burning

> as long as one of us tends a fire
> all of us can borrow

she only asks that we
do not disturb her good hearth

she needs just enough fire
to feel the truth cook

> to see what she is doing
> what she is truly doing
> not what she wishes to think she is doing

I visit carefully
I do not disturb her good hearth

onto the burning husks
I gently place a handful of straw, enough
just enough
for one small burst
of light.

THESE THINGS, THAT OTHERS MIGHT CALL MIRACLES

And here I am, trembling over white wine in a waterfront restaurant
found by this investigative angel on a mission of deliverance
I love that she is as nervous as me, doesn't ask me to explain
the wounding event, the adoption of thirty years ago, I love that

she has her father's hair, only on her it's sun-lit and wheaten
and she has my deep-set eyes though burnished in gentle green
and looking at me, loving me, she says she has always loved me
even the humped and heavy memory of my bending shadow
this young lady, my daughter, has loved even my phantom

we declare each other in a claim that rises and cuts
through the immediate like the blade of an old, old dagger
that her hands lift from its self-plunge into my soul
it is her grasp that draws it forth like Excalibur from rock
—carefully, as a garden rake pulled from a manatee's back
—mouse gently, as a bristly splinter from a lion's injured paw

she lifts it aloft, exposes it as the sharp-edged monstrance it is
and in one pure glittering motion, one solemn wave
she slashes the cataract of heaven's eye

and here I am in a swirl of released stars of white fog
that pour down, tumble down on air-white wings of recognitions
first-born sensations, I remember, recognize, and it is all in this moment
more glistening than imagined, this moment that holds all other moments
on the pier in front of a waterside restaurant, it is all in this moment
that these things, that others may call miracles, fall on me
fall on me, and make me more.

THE PONDEROUS FALLS FROM HER

She knows pilots don't fall out of open cockpits
even when the plane turns sideways or flips

forward momentum holds body against seat
firmly enough to counter gravity's pull

knows for the vermouth of foreign, streaming skies
to move over her like cosmic oceans of wine
there is such a thing as being too careful

if she gives in to her fears, if she believes she is insufficient
if she doesn't push gently against pictures of what has been learned
then discarded, the edges cut off and the rest mutilated
she will turn around too early, each time she will turn back sooner
one day she will turn back before take-off

knows how weakness fossilizes in the heart
works as a weight against flight, jams her lift to leave
knows about bravery and why she must keep flying
into wildernesses of mirrors hung with still-wet paintings
of instrument gauges, must keep flying until the ponderous
falls from her, caught like an insect in resin, honey-lit
at its center, all she doesn't know she's hidden

and finally, amber of heart, she will begin her slow descent
to the dark and cluttered landing strip, that, seeing her approach
will rise up brilliant with her flaws, blazing with her defects
and all lit up to welcome her.

WILD GLASS

I wear what I do six inches above my head
like a crackly halo of consciousness

all that matters is dark halves turned up to whole bright
that opens itself to outcome, gives
I cannot hold it, all this giving

can only cup my ear to the air in a delirium rite
hear the warm wax of time melt into noon where I scribble
that for which I was born, sculpt words
as the brook rushes the rock
as leaves fall to mulch

and it is how I shape language that strikes my life
breaks it down, spell its name
fills my spare, sparse heart
with invitations, makes room for the voice
the gift to speak through me
in what I do

And what I do is write, write out what was hidden
dormant, make possible what can't be managed
in a pierce too keen to be felt, I peel back the day
like skin into a perfect night charged with stars

where one bright brooch of moon folds into its mold
each effort, each thought of mine like heavenly gold cream
that I can drink, can sip like a last bit of fire

like work that is good, from this diamond cut
wild glass of self.

AS A TROBRIAND ISLANDER HARVESTS YAMS

East of New Guinea, the concept of tubers expands
everyday language and is sung into consecrated food
with sacred regard for the multiplicity of beingness
because in the soul of the yam garden
any attribute that changes any life is identified
and retained and named:

taytu they call these yams which round themselves ripely to
the tips without spiky points or rotten spots, unlike a *bwanawa*
improper in its ripeness; if overripe, they explain, it is a *yowana*
if blighted, a *nuunokuna*; when new tubers have formed, a *gadena*.

Beloved, as a Trobriand Islander harvests yams
gather what you yield and carefully discern
the starchy tuberous root of all the beings you are
receive your beautifully blighted, misshapen spots
tenderly connected within the moment's particular flesh
in an achingly sensitive basket of appreciation

I identify and retain and name and sing all that you are
into a eucharistic feast of the highest authenticity
for in collecting and preparing such extreme crops
I am spiritually explained, blessed and increased.

ANTIQUE SHOP

Against the rain
display windows are sealed shut
lace clothed, silver-fringed tables heap
with pigeon blood goblets
china doll faces, garnet clasped shawls
a round glass paperweight confines a single
perfect hyacinth, suspended, buried alive
all the air squeezed out
I too cannot breathe, inhale ashes of roses
freshly snuffed beeswax candles
dust of crushed, dried lavender
powdered fungus, old spores
it is not the steam rising from my raincoat
suffocates, it is the glass ball
breathing without breath
the impending death of a friend, of me
I enter without resistance the enfolding mildew
plans within plans
known human imprints
someone else's past haunted and hovering
I am no longer browsing customer
I am host.

THE WAY OUR DREAMS SWAM IN SYNC

We can do this at least, remember
how we were in love with Esther Williams
forcing ourselves to smile like she did
in spite of our eyes burning
from chlorine chops of splashed water

practicing turnovers that took us to the bottom
of things, believing everything turns around
at the end, our wispy hair popping out from under
our caps in tufts and clumps, telling each other
how pretty we were

after the whistle blew and everyone got out
shivering in cold stall showers
we dared ourselves to hide behind the lockers
until the echoes of whistles and voices ricocheting
from cement walls and the entire building cleared out

dared ourselves to slip just us into the lapis blue
gelatin, bodies like mermaids, cause no ripples
or splashes, red hibiscus in our loosened hair
being lifted up and out of the underwater lights
by a helicopter manned with movie cameras
fountains erupting at our feet up to the orchid
garlanded swing where we lean and point our toes

but we just talked, then dressed with the others
hiding behind towels, dabbing Blue Waltz toilet water
behind our ears (that's how our mothers taught us)
we covered our wet ponytails in identical white scarves
applied more Flame-Glo pale pink lipstick
over the darkening reddish-blue it had become
saved our bus fare so we could walk to Woolworth's
and cram ourselves into the hollow box and pose
for the photo flash, pucker, stick out our tongues
slide on the tiny plastic seat, fall upon each other
giddy, crazy, laughing, crying, almost peeing our pants

well, more than almost, but that was many lives ago
many girlhoods ago, today we dribble with each cough
or sneeze or unexpected spurt of laughter
husbands dead, children gone, hardly any of us remain
we find each other, try to resume where we left off

it seems we have learned much too competently
much too acutely, how to live alone, how to measure
how to avoid other people's hells, save a buck, do without
the kind of friends you just goof around with, can't
remember the last time we caught an old Esther Williams
movie on television; the vanilla scent of cheap toilet water
in heart-shaped bottles; the way our dreams swam in sync

oh we try, but to the whiff of chlorine that comes like
the phantom aroma of snuffed candles one can sense emitting
from a cassette tape of monks chanting just finished and turned off
finally one of us becomes sensible about underwater somersaults
and how they come up from under to go over, and over
until they are definitely over, one of us honors the pragmatic
and politely, firmly, asks about grandchildren.

IN TIME, EVEN GHOSTS CAN HEAL

Tonight is one of those nights
I go back and forth between conclusions
the kind like barnacles found in the armpits
of seals that sleep on my pier

I open my window, no stars emerge
over the night sea, the dark comes and goes
clouds drift above, brood, pout like injured ghosts
call to mind someone, maybe you, long dead
who I might have plundered and rendered

I am wretched in my need to apologize
for how I swaggered, daring you to touch, be touched
making love without love, no I was not busy
when you came to forgive me, I was not even preparing
to be busy, that's the armor I put on to pretend
I had a purpose in the world, oh how I curse
my young arrogance for telling you that, spitefully
—a long time ago I knew everything

now all I want to do is make what is uneven, even
wrap myself in a night-blue velvet robe
arranging it in serpentine folds at my bare feet
want to stroke the earth with consideration
cast smooth the things that hide; comfort the weeping
caused by my inept and thoughtless words

this is one of those nights I stay with myself
(it always starts with simply being alone with the alone)
until my regret sheds from the moon
like thin silver blood down the sorry, sorry slope
of my exposed throat, at last

the night sky understands; this then is my life's work
my visible art that reveals mistakes and instigates
further invention; what is done, is done, nevertheless
in time even ghosts can heal, their essences settling darkly
over the softest muffle of the sighing, forgiving sea.

NOT THE FIRST UNBELIEVER
1. SEDONA

I wore a modest nightgown most of the time, white cotton
with a bit of blue ribbon around the neckline, it doesn't matter she says
wants me to forgive him because she loves him, brings me to Sedona
a mother-daughter geology of electromagnetic vortexes, entries
exits of energy on tap, she wants me to give him another chance
change the reading of what has been set in motion
and it is a huge sweep of iron-red fault that creates this canyon
powders us with a fine red dust of dried menstrual blood

he pierced hidden peepholes between my bed and bath, I argue
crouched at them in the dark, watched me rub a towel between my thighs
barefoot in the backseat of my girlishness, I was racehorse quality
wearing my wildling mouth like nothing more than warm summer evenings
and I caught him, I ran back for the forgotten shampoo and I caught him
and I want to know, demand to know, what you are going to do about it

but he is in recovery, in therapy, changed, no longer like that
you must understand I'm going to marry him

the afternoon sun lights up a rock formation
behind her head in russet and gold, her face recedes into shadow
and the erotic comes to mind, she is with him, even now, in his decomposition
and I am used up, heavy with hotness of vacant space, air thick with smells
of burning rock that rises from this flowerless mountain, I turn from the heat
of her eyes, have to look away from her eyes that burn as though someone
has put a match to them and they are wide, smoldering coals of garnet.

NOT THE FIRST UNBELIEVER
2. THE WEDDING

Only I can tell they made love just before leaving
it's the way he slips his fingers from her damp armpit
to burrow under the peach strap of her seersucker sundress
as he hand-walks her around the wedding reception

no one is sure who else knows what he did to me
my mother wants support for this union, wants me here
where everyone else looks for behavior instructions
from his turtleheaded mother who always speaks
what is best for others and thinks the low attendance
at this wedding is because of the rain

I will ease myself back into myself a little bit more
each day, can pretend he has been forgiven, can deceive him
as he did me, as he does my mother

he thinks he has something to do with my world
takes my elbow with one white-knuckled hand
bustles and shoves me towards his side of the family
who in-kind turn into the core of their own band, into gossip
watching sideways to allow us to put on the show

doesn't know his grasp is all that holds him to me
reciting clever platitudes, little sayings of talk-show therapists

this morning I put my hand and forehead on the cold window glass
tried to pull my spirit back, but the thought of him returned
there is still my handprint on the windowpane, the mark
of someone trying to reach another world, the mark of someone
who belongs to no one, without blessing or need to be blessed.

NOT THE FIRST UNBELIEVER
    3. FIREBOAT

We watch the harbor fireboat spew and pump its show
twenty thousand gallons per minute hose down the sky

you put your hand against the silver-blue corona
look into a heaven alive with star sapphires

want me to help you identify, prove the direction you travel in
recognize and refute the miracle of your god
and then shape your deep, deep connection into something else

in the drag of its fire-gilt arcs you look for the possibility
of extending, drawing out and enlarging the only force
that could have made such a mess of your life

you are not the first unbeliever who wants to see the Virgin Mary
in garage door stains, Elvis alive, signs in crop circles
Princess Diana's face in storm clouds

in the thrown net of all your sticky thoughts you insist
there must be much more to this than just harbor fireboat spray

you squint for a vision, want the picture to gush its image through
as an explanation for the script you comply with
if it exists at all, it cannot be human
you cannot have consummated your own ruin all by yourself

as you blabber away, the fireboat stops casting out its spirits
I scan the sky of pale water washed blue of liabilities
and there is not a devil in sight.

OTHERTHINGS

Unshaded cows dumbly swish the heat
the strewn straw, the dust.

Concentration-camped, they munch
long forgetting
there could be something else.

My ancestors drank blood from skulls
with no dilution, plunging pagan spirits
into trees and animals, stickily
as heated honey.

A castrated bull turns to the fence
and moos like a cow.

I sicken with sun overdose,
smokeless firepit smells.

There are otherthings I must remember.

I thirst.

PARAKEET EXPECTATIONS

She of the stone-wart on her deformed beak
old yellow and chartreuse, always on her perch
primly set on a seriously important mission
would watch him, young, sky-blue with a necklace
of miniature black baroque pearls
fly to my shoulder, nip my earrings
act the boy, bathe in my cupped hands
under the running cold-water faucet, splash,
squawk outrageously

he died folding in as I held him to my heart
and not much later, she died, slowly
one wing spread on the bottom of the cage
angrily pecking my hand to the last

neither damaged me with expectations
nor burdened me with personal light or darkness

from behind their bars,
they had set me free
to cry copiously at their death and link
all things I had always thought of as opposite

we buried her beside him, in the backyard
under the beech tree dripping with nests
where brown-gray birds teach their fat babies
how to fly and hop and stir up fallen leafy bits

and I wonder how we will all finish up
not knowing until the moment after it has happened
I wonder, and in their auras shadowed on the graves
I can sometimes see Fra Angelico angels
a whole, brilliant, flapping rapture of them.

INSINUATION OF WINGS

Of how when bowing, bending to examine the aerodynamics
found in the light puff of a cockroach wing frozen mosquito-like
in the filament of an electric light bulb, the blades of our shoulders
like wings, point up to swans and condors obsessed with their own flying

what are we but infatuated, earthbound, flightless beings
who for generations have reconfigured how they might be
if we were to have wings, imagining pigeon or gull feathers
incense-smoke gray, albino bat wings, crackling tracing paper
unconsecrated dried communion wafers; old parchment
fierce skin stretched taut across salt-white digits of hind forelimbs
or blind eyelids sketched with velvet veins pulled over
what would have to be thin, hollow bird bones, oh these bones

we grow old, we contemplate our own bones and angel wings
like those of the Seraphim, three sets that open from their backs
our thick, heavy skeletons disintegrate, bend us over as we move
force us to bow to flight even as earth-wrapped, we hunch in our chairs
to study aeronautics, our shoulder blades pointing even sharper
upward to where flight belongs, even so, unfocused and unfanged
our yearning comes not from our own physical insinuation of wings
but from the heart-contracting energy that ardently pulls us toward it.

AQUARIA

Sun is trapped in the surface above us
in the glare-streaked monastic-library dark of aquaria
filtered like inquiring voices of children and grown-ups
that blend to a uniform murmur, a subhuman drone
of distant choirs that plunge fish-lit shafts of daylight
into visual hosannas, the meanings of which escape me
the essences of which form like cubes of water

deference is duly paid to the ceiling of light
to the unseen, unimaginable brightness
through and above windows that float on black walls
foreign sources of necessary surprises, sea sights
of green and gold illuminations, spangled flesh
transfinite flashes of benevolent silver fishtails
that trail like aquatic comets, sharks, urchins
gatherers of barnacles, great beginnings
where the ends of things are always present

perhaps I deify these hinged mouths and milky eyes
wise as shipwrecks, glorifying all microscopic
sacrosanct, glitter-lit flutterings that achieve
darting levels of enigma, of motion so fast
they seem to be racing winks of air bubbles
swimming from shells to be cloned as cells
—schools of souls streaking holy with honor
for their moist birthing from a cold-blooded goddess

mercifully, no one asks if I need help
and I am allowed to gradually diminish, to browse
to respect hints of ocean floors lit by torrid noons

I am left alone to take heed, grapple with reflections
attain prismatic states of high lightness
understand what it was I tried so hard to contemplate
in convent churches and patriarchal cathedrals
doing at last in an unconsecrated crypt what I once called
for lack of any ability to see into things, praying.

ABOUT THE AUTHOR

Eileen Malone's poetry has been published in over four hundred literary journals and anthologies, a significant amount of which have earned prestigious awards. She taught for San Francisco Bay Area California Community Colleges, and for the California Poetry in the Schools Program. Eileen Malone founded the Soul-Making Literary Competition in 1994 and continues to direct and coordinate its annual Awards Event.

THE RAGGED SKY POETRY SERIES

Susquehanna and *The Confidence Man* by Michael R. Brown

The Luxury of Obstacles by Elizabeth Danson

Little Knitted Sister by Ellen Foos

Loose Parlance by Daniel A. Harris

Moonmilk and Other Poems by Carlos Hernández Peña

Eating Her Wedding Dress: A Collection of Clothing Poems edited by Katsarou, O'Toole, and Foos

Dog Watch by Valerie Lawson

I Should Have Given Them Water by Eileen Malone

Between Silence and Praise by Elizabeth Anne Socolow

Penguins in a Warming World by Anca Vlasopolos

Escape Velocity by Arlene Weiner